BECAUSE

A Tale of Two Loves

BECAUSE: A Tale of Two Loves
Copyright © 2024 by Carla Atkinson

Published in the United States of America

Library of Congress Control Number: 2024918031
ISBN   Paperback: 979-8-89091-719-5
ISBN   Hardback: 979-8-89091-720-1
ISBN   eBook: 979-8-89091-721-8

All rights reserved. No part of this publication may be reproduced, stored in a retrieval system or transmitted in any way by any means, electronic, mechanical, photocopy, recording or otherwise without the prior permission of the author except as provided by USA copyright law.

The opinions expressed by the author are not necessarily those of ReadersMagnet, LLC.

ReadersMagnet, LLC
10620 Treena Street, Suite 230 | San Diego, California, 92131 USA
1.619.354.2643 | www.readersmagnet.com

Book design copyright © 2024 by ReadersMagnet, LLC. All rights reserved.

Cover design by Jhiee Oraiz
Interior design by Daniel Lopez

BECAUSE

A Tale of Two Loves

Carla Atkinson

INTRODUCTION

I wrote this book to answer the questions so many people have asked me: "WHY" is the question. Why did you choose to parent over 200 children over a 50 year period? Where did you get the patience? Where did you get the energy? How did your marriage survive?

The answer is BECAUSE. I chose to answer that question with the story of a love handed down to us by my parents Dale and Nellie Marr (whom I refer to as "He" and "She" in the story), and our savior Jesus Christ. Love comes in many ways. In my life it came through a never ending source of commitment, humor, deep caring, mercy, and understanding. Add to this the desire to understand trauma and the education and training to not only deal with it but live with it.

TABLE OF CONTENTS

Introduction v

Chapter One: *SHE* 1

Chapter Two: *HE* 13

Chapter Three: *The List* 21

Chapter Four: *Silly Ole' Dad* 25

Chapter Five: *The Blessing* 29

Chapter Six: *I Loved Him For That* 35

Chapter Seven: *Why Carla* 47

Chapter Eight: *In Jesus Name* 55

CHAPTER 1

SHE

BECAUSE, I believe the great values

SHE handed down, the never

ending patience SHE had for this hyper-active

person (in the days they didn't medicate children),

and the terrific love affair of my parents,

set me on my course in life.

Carla Atkinson

SHE was my mom!

She was a kind, patient and loving person to all who came into her life. Her whole life was dedicated to serving the Lord by doing things for others. Her family and her church family came first, but she had an open heart for anyone who needed a helping hand, or a hug, or a smile.

Everything she did, she did well. She made all of our clothes when we were children. I was the only girl, and in those days, girls were expected to wear dresses. She not only kept me in the most fashionable dresses, but she made my nightgowns and bathrobes. When I performed in a piano recital she even made me a formal gown. She made our Halloween costumes, and we often won awards for them.

For my dad and brothers, she made shirts. At that time, the most popular style was Pendleton shirts so she went to the factory, bought the fabric, and made them herself. She even made my dad's ties. He was a large man and store-bought ties were never quite long enough for him. She made ties that fit him perfectly. Sometimes when he was on an airplane someone would stop him and ask, "Where did you get that tie? I can never find one long enough." "Oh, my wife makes them for me." He would reply, and then he'd offer, "You want it? Here, take it! She will make me another one, and she always did!" My husband Jim and I had a large family of two natural, three adopted, and approximately two hundred foster children throughout 45 years. She made dresses for every girl, and cowboy outfits and shirts for all who wanted them.

She was a wonderful cook and also made amazing baked goods. She made a personal cake for each child's birthday, and made a special dinner for every festive occasion. Since my dad loved apple pie, she baked one for him every day.

BECAUSE: A Tale of Two Loves

She could make a garden thrive and grow. Her vegetables were plentiful and beautiful, but her flowers were spectacular. When the country club was planning an event, it wouldn't be surprising for the decoration team to show up at her house and ask, "How do you do it? Your flowers are always so beautiful!" "Do you want some for your tables?" she would ask, and then she would cut whatever they wanted for their occasion. She grew, picked, and arranged two bouquets of flowers for our church every week during our growing up years.

She made something for every person she knew. At Christmas time we'd see her make thirty shirts at a time. She just loved to bless her family and friends. When she died, three hundred and fifty people came to her funeral, and every one spontaneously wore something she had personally made them.

The most amazing thing about her was the way she lived her life. While she was a rather quiet, almost shy person, who never liked to be in the spotlight, she was a person of deep beliefs and strong, clearcut choices.

My dad believed she should be an independent woman, which was contrary to popular beliefs back then. He supported her in the things she loved to do and together they agreed she would flourish as a stay-at-home wife and mother.

She believed that everyone should always attempt to do their best and that is what she expected of us, as well as what she taught us. We never appeared anywhere with holes in our clothes. She either mended them or discarded them. She believed we should dress in our best clothes for church. She said, "We show God our thankfulness for the gift of Jesus by presenting ourselves for worship in our best attire."

Carla Atkinson

She taught us to respect our father who worked hard for us. When we were young, he worked in highway construction. His work exposed him to the elements, and was often dangerous. She believed we should honor him for his hard work and sacrifice. We came in from play in time to bathe, put on clean clothes, and to comb our hair before he came home from work. He came home to a clean, well-ordered home, clean children, and the table set for a three-course meal. She allowed no cartons, jars, packages or cans on the table. Every night she set up a proper table.

There was no bickering at our table. Everyone was given an opportunity to share their day but we were allowed however, and even encouraged, to disagree, or even argue – BUT – it better not be disrespectful.

There was no end to the wonder of that woman!

When I got married, she made my wedding dress. I explained what I wanted. She designed it, ordered French lace from France, (before we even had internet), and made the dress. She also made 9 bridesmaid dresses, her dress, and the dresses for my two grandmothers.

She believed Christmas should be celebrated because of the wonderful gift we'd received in Jesus. She decided a year in advance, she'd what she would make for each person. She listened carefully to what they wanted, went to the store to look at it, and then came home and made it herself.

We called her the "Queen", because our father held her in such high esteem. When he retired, he said, "She has served me with her whole heart and with her whole life, and now it's my turn to serve her." He was by her side for the rest of her life. I have truly had a blessed life because SHE was my mother.

BECAUSE: A Tale of Two Loves

BECAUSE this little memory my mother wrote was the

best way I could show you the love my parents had for each other.

The line she wrote, "Oh I would have believed him anyway",

as well as the lines in the last paragraph, show the

depth of their admiration for each other.

Carla Atkinson

Dinner at the White House
January 14th 1981

In my father's later years, he became Business Manager of Operating Engineers Local #3. He was also a leading world renown expert on mining and construction safety. Because of this he often worked with foreign heads of state as well as two United States Presidents. After a dinner at the White House, she wrote this memoir:

Last night we had dinner at the "WHITE HOUSE"!!! We, Dale and Nellie Marr, had dinner at the White House with the PRESIDENT OF THE UNITED STATES OF AMERICA!!!

Never, in our wildest expectations, when we met and fell in love as young teenagers in 1933, did we ever imagine that anything like this would happen to us! Yet, as I look back on our 43 years of marriage, I realize that I have had such complete trust in Dale's ability to accomplish anything he set out to do. In 1937 when we married and he told me, "Someday I will take you to dinner at the White House with the President of the United States." Surprisingly, I actually believed him and expected it to happen.

It was a wonderful, thrilling, unbelievable evening from beginning to end and I shall never forget it! The anticipation over the past two weeks since we accepted the invitation had been exciting. But that was nothing compared to the butterflies in my stomach when we actually started to get dressed yesterday afternoon. Dale often accused me of always being late. Not yesterday! I started to dress at 4:15 P.M., and was all ready to go at 5:00 pm. Jay and Mary Turner were picking us up in the International's Limousine at 5:45 P.M. We sat and looked at each other with admiring smiles until 5:20 P.M., and then we went down to the lobby to wait for them. When they arrived, we went first to the International Headquarters of A.F.L. to attend a reception for the Secretary of Labor, Ray Marshall.

We were to arrive at the White House at 7:30P.M., but Jay wanted to be early so he could park and leave the limousine so the driver could go home. We arrived just before 7:00 P.M. and the guard at the gate asked us to wait for a short while. The lights were on in the White House and so were the flood lights on the grounds. There was some snow on the ground and it was a beautiful and, I thought, serene sight when so much controversy was swirling around the world.

Soon the gates were opened and we were allowed to drive up (Southwest Gate) the driveway near the entrance to the White House. We were amongst the first ones to arrive. We checked our coats and Mary and I went to the lady's room to look in the mirror and see if we would pass inspection in our own minds eyes!

Uniformed, polite and smiling guards met us as we arrived. We were requested to stay downstairs until 7:30 P.M. We enjoyed the time by looking through the library, enjoying the objects of art, the pictures, the paintings, and the portraits. We noticed the one of "Jackie" that said "Jacqueline Kennedy Onassis". We wondered why they had added the "Onassis", and we wondered if she were to remarry, if they would add another name!?

At 7:30 P.M. we were escorted up the winding marble stairway to the main floor. There we walked by the Marine Band that was playing for us, and down the hallway on the red carpet to the "East Room". There, as we entered the room, we were announced over the loud speaker system. "MR. AND MRS.

DALE MARR!" - I thought – "That's Us" – Mr. and Mrs. Middle America" – Aspirations to be good Christians, Good Parents, Good Citizens – here at the White House to have dinner with the President and First Lady of "Our Country!"

That room was the scene of a reception until 8:15 P.M., when the band began to play "Hail to the Chief" and the President and Mrs. Carter arrived, along with the Vice President and Mrs. Mondale. Until they arrived, guests were served glasses of rose or white wine or champagne or orange juice for us "teetotalers". We saw and visited with friends and met new people. All were from Labor Circles. International Presidents – Secretary of Labor Marshall and some of his assistants. John Henning and his wife were the only other people there from California. Lance Kirkland, President of A.F.L. and his wife – Bobby Georginer, President of the Building Trades – Dale can name many others. He knew many of them personally. We also took note of the beauty of the room. Very large portraits of George and Martha Washington hung on either sides of a stage or platform that was raised several feet. There was a grand piano on the platform. They say it is the one President Truman used to play. Around the platform was a solid bank of live greenery. Amongst that were dozens of sprays of Butterfly Orchids. In every room that we were in, and on every table, there were <u>huge</u> bouquets of fresh flowers. They were beautiful!

When the President and the Vice President and their wives arrived, they stood and shook hands with each one of us. We were told to give them our full names as we shook their hands. Even though we had met them and shook their hands before, it was still an exciting experience. I'm sure if the President and Mrs. Carter met me today on the street, they would not remember ever seeing me before, and yet I feel as though I have known them well and for

BECAUSE: A Tale of Two Loves

a long time. I have liked them as the President and First Lady. I think they have served our country well! I'm sorry they don't have another four years to complete the plans they have made.

We went into the Dining Room for dinner. There were ten people seated at each table, and we thought there were 12 or 14 tables. The Carters were two tables away from us on one side of the room center, and the Mondales were at a table on the other side. We had place cards and we were surprised to see that Dale was the HOST at our table. The dinner and the service, which came in courses, was very elegant! The china and the silver were beautiful. We had a bouquet of white tulips, roses, and carnations on our table.

The first course was trout stuffed with shrimp, crab, etc., hot rolls and butter. Then roast prime rib and green beans. Then a green salad with sliced cheese (different than our salads before the main course). Fingerbowls next. Dessert was chocolate mousse. It had been molded and looked like a picture. Petit Fours also. Dishes of chocolate mints – and, of course, peanuts!

The dinner conversation was interesting. The Turners were the only ones at our table who had attended a dinner at the White House before. We all thought it was pretty wonderful. We thought the room was beautiful. Dale and I remarked about the beautiful chandeliers there and in the East Room. We remembered being so impressed with the ones we saw in the Palaces in Europe. We decided these were just as beautiful. Behind the place where President Carter sat hung a very large and beautiful portrait of Abraham Lincoln. Under it was an inscription (not on the picture, but on the fireplace) by President James Adams – praying God's blessings on all who enter this house.

President Carter spoke when he was finished eating. He said many important people had been served dinner in that room. Many presidents, kings, queens, shahs, heads of state etc., but he didn't think there had been that many presidents in that room at one time. He asked for all the presidents to raise their hands and there were a lot of them! Vice President Mondale spoke and said Secretary of Labor Marshall was the best Secretary of Labor this Country ever had. We all agreed. Lance Kirkland spoke and proposed a toast to President Carter. That called for a standing ovation and prolonged clapping.

We were invited back into the East Room for some entertainment. (I left out a very important part of our dinner. The Marine Violinist played for us as they strolled amongst our tables. There were many of them and it was beautiful). As we went from the dining room to the East Room, the Marine Band was playing. Some of the people stopped to dance. Some stopped and talked to the Carters and the Mondales. I would have liked to talk to them, but there were so many people crowded around them, so we went on in to get a front row seat for the entertainment. I would have liked to thank the President and Mrs. Carter for their dedication in serving our country with dignity and loyalty, not only to our country, but to our Lord and Savior. I appreciate the fact that they served prayerfully. Dale and I understand that because prayer is so much a part of our lives. I wanted to thank them for being our President and First Lady!

In the East Room we were to be entertained by John Raitt, the singer. He came and sat down by us and began a conversation. When Dale told him we were from San Francisco, he said he would be there Saturday night. He would be singing in the telethon for Cerebral Palsy. He said he began his career in San Francisco. He said he had sung a lot of places but, never in the White House. This was a first and he, too, was thrilled. President Carter introduced John

BECAUSE: A Tale of Two Loves

Raitt. He said 35 years ago he was in New York for the first time. He was in the Navy with a pay of $7.50 per month. He took half of that salary and went to a Broadway musical. It was Carousel and John Raitt sang the lead. He had never attended anything like that before and he was so impressed, he would never forget it. He had followed John Raitt's career through the years and had invited him there to sing for us. He sang songs from Carousel, Oklahoma, Pajama Game and Shenandoah. It was marvelous. When he had finished, President and Mrs. Carter said "Good Night". Everyone hated for the evening to end. The Marine band was playing again. John Raitt sang some more with them.

We looked in some of the other rooms. There was a roaring fire in each room. We looked out the windows for a long time at the view across the Tidal Basin at the Washington Monument and the Jefferson Memorial. Both were covered with flood lights. The ground was white with snow – Tidal Basin covered with ice – but it was a warm magnificent site.

We listened to the Marine Band for a while and then, reluctantly, we left with Mary and Jay for our hotel. We all agreed it was a wonderful evening and one we would never forget!

Funny thing happened – when we were at dinner, I looked across the table at Dale and thought how handsome he looked. I looked all around the room and thought to myself, "There is not another man in the room that is as handsome as he is!!" When we were ion our room, Dale said to me, "Honey, I was very proud of you tonight. I looked around the room and decided you were the most attractive woman there!!"

I thanked him for taking me and for the wonderful evening, and then my emotions caught up with me….and I cried!!!!

CHAPTER 2

HE

BECAUSE I want you to understand the overflowing

love and security of not only a good father,

but the example of a good husband.

Carla Atkinson

My Dad, HE was my HERO!

With him we all felt safe. If you were to ask anyone who knew him to describe him in one word, it would be "Character". He was quite the character. He had strong beliefs, especially in family, religion, politics, and loyalty.

When he was a child, his family was extremely poor. They walked several miles to school with no soles in their shoes. He was a prideful child, as he was as a man. He was never ashamed to be poor. Their badge of honor was that their mother was beautiful. She never cut her hair and it was very long and beautiful. When he was eleven years old his family ran out of food. They were even out of the potatoes they had grown. His mother left home, went to town, and came back with her hair completely cut off to her ears. The money she made from selling her hair provided food for a year. He decided her could never eat that food.

At eleven years old he ran away from home. From Battlecreek, Washington to Portland, Oregon. He was a large, older looking child, and he got a job immediately as a parking attendant at a gambling casino. He slept in the park until the owner found out and offered him the kiosk to sleep in. He made a deal with the owner that as long as he stayed in school, he could stay for free. As he earned money, he sent home for each member of his family.

He bought a car when he was eighteen years old, and while his brother was trying it out, a drunk driver ran a stop sign and hit his side of the car. By this time, he and my mother were planning a wedding. He had a bid to play professional baseball as a catcher. This accident put a stop to all of that.

He got Osteomyelitis in his right hip and he laid in the hospital for a year and a half. Since there was no cure for this infection he was expected to die.

BECAUSE: A Tale of Two Loves

At this time Penicillin was made public as an experimental medication. They gave him the Penicillin and it saved his life.

He couldn't work because at this time the economy was decimated as a result of the crash of 1929. He and my mother had married and had a son. Most men of that day were on what was called the "dole". He said, "I will never stand in that line".

He hitchhiked to California and got a job on the docks. With his first paycheck he had a train ticket for my mother, a flat above the grocery store, and a dollar fifty in his pocket. He hitchhiked back to Oregon, put my mother and brother on the train, and then hitchhiked back to California.

He was a strong union man from the start. His union had lost autonomy due to mismanagement. He believed "A man ought to be able to work an honest day for an honest day's wage. His wife ought to be able to have her babies in a hospital, and his kids should be able to see a dentist and a doctor." He was determined to work this out in his union. He carried a tire iron and a heavy chain to union meetings because he had to fight his way out. He stood up for the working man and from that point on, for the rest of his life, he always did.

He became Business Manager for Operating Engineers Local #3, a vice president for the International Union, and a world renown construction and mining safety expert. Both Republican and Democratic Presidents sought his advice, as did heads of many countries and states.

Above all he was my Dad. Most construction workers of the day followed the jobs. They lived in trailers, and their families were constantly on the move. He and my mother chose to buy a house. Then, he followed the work, came home on weekends, and we stayed in one place. He fixed things, helped with yard work, entertained friends at large dinners, took the family to fun places, and entertained all with his stories. He did more on the weekends than most men did all week.

He and my mother had a great romance. They played, laughed, and loved each other openly. We really loved it when his job was close enough to home that he came home every night.

Every summer, from the day the snow melted to the day school started, we moved to the mountains with him. He worked on the highway following the Yuba River every summer repairing the damage done due to the heavy winters. Those were carefree days for us because we left the regimen of fall and winter behind.

He believed in the Lord Jesus Christ. He and my mother chose to take us to church every Wednesday night for prayer meeting and bible study, and every Sunday morning and evening for worship. He served on the Board of Deacons for many years.

In those days the pastor lived in a parsonage and when retired moved to a home for retired pastors. He objected to this arrangement. He believed a pastor should have an adequate salary so he could afford to buy his own house and retire with something of his own. He was always a forward thinker.

He was a staunch Democrat, and stood behind democratic candidates with all his might and influence. We went with him on marches, political rallies, and fund raisers. During the time when Jerry Brown was Governor he gave Jerry Brown a very hard time even though he helped get him elected. He disapproved of the way Brown lived and because he had longer hair, he called him a "rag head" to his face. When he died, Jerry Brown came to the funeral and stood to speak, "I just had to come pay honor to the man who called me a rag head." he said.

He believed in loyalty. When he was the head of the union, he and my mother officiated at many functions. They vowed to never drink alcohol and never dance with anyone else. They avoided many of the marital problems other people, in similar positions had because of their choices.

We always had Heinz Ketchup, Folgers Coffee, and Gillette products in our house because they sponsored the sports shows he watched on TV and listened to on the radio. He supported our school and clubs, the union, and the church because he believed in loyalty.

Any story about him isn't complete without mentioning his many sayings. He quoted these at various occasions sometimes to the amusement of family and friends and sometimes to their dismay.

- In cold weather,
    - "It was colder than a well diggers fanny".
- When something was lost,
    - "He/she couldn't find their fanny in a phone booth with both hands".
- When my mother couldn't decide on a restaurant,
    - "Good God Kid, my stomach's so hungry it thinks my throat's been cut".
- When someone threw something and missed the target,
    - "He/she couldn't hit a bull in the fanny with a barn door".

Although he was originally dismayed when we began taking so many children, he whole heartedly accepted each one. One time, when we took in our fifth child, he met that 6 year old for the first time at one of our family birthday parties. One of the little boys got a Big Wheel for his birthday. Our new child was so excited that his "brother" got such a nice gift that he jumped up and down and patted the brother on the back. That melted my dad's heart. "Here", he said, as he handed me fifty dollars. "Go buy that little guy a Big Wheel. Look at how happy he is for someone else". Ten minutes later he said to me, "Punk, did you find one? Did you get that kid a Big Wheel yet?"

"No dad! It's six pm Sunday. Nothing is open!

Ten AM Monday morning I got a call, "Punk, you got that kid a Big Wheel yet?" That's how he was, always thinking and doing for others.

There is no end to stories that could be told about him and his life. Suffice it to say simply, he was my HERO.

CHAPTER 3

THE LIST

BECAUSE this was a significant event in my life:

BECAUSE it started me on the road

of making good choices.

Carla Atkinson

When I was twelve my dad called me aside and said, "Punk, you are a difficult woman and I don't want to spend your teenage years fighting with you over boys."

"Here is what I want you to do. I want you to make a list of what you want in a date, a boyfriend, and a husband. What do you expect in a relationship? Then when you want to go on a date, don't ever come to me and ask if you can go on a date? Come to me with the list and show me how that person matches your list. If it's a match, you can go."

Although all my friends were having boyfriends at fifteen, I didn't. In fact, I didn't have a date until the Junior Prom because no one matched my list.

Here are some of the things on my list at twelve years of age:

1. No sports
2. Had to be a Christian
3. Had to treat his family well, especially his mother
4. Had to have a sense of humor and laugh a lot
5. No one who peeled out of the parking lot
6. Had to like children
7. Had to like animals
8. Wasn't a jealous person
9. Someone who liked going to movies.

When Jim called, he said, "This is Jim. I want to know if you would go to the junior prom with me?"

I didn't answer right away because in my mind I was checking my list. He said it again, "I want to know if you would go to the junior prom with me?"

Me – still checking, no answer!

Jim – "Well would you, or wouldn't you?"

Me – "Well then, I guess I will" and then I hung up.

That was the first date in 1958. We married in 1961. To date we have been married for 63 years.

CHAPTER 4

SILLY OLE' DAD

I actually wrote this piece many years ago

BECAUSE I wanted to share with our children

and grandchildren memories that

we all treasure.

Carla Atkinson

I think I am one of the most blessed people on earth. I was raised in a Christian family with family values, community values, national values and personal values. I was raised by encouraging parents who helped me believe I could do anything I really wanted to do. They taught me how to dream, set goals, evaluate and appreciate the things I accomplished.

My Mom taught me how to be competent and master any job I set out to do. She taught me determination, quality, and the sheer pleasure in using and expanding my capabilities.

It was my Dad however, who put the 'icing on the cake'. He put a little bit of the ridiculous into life. After a day of working in the yard, he would say, "Anybody interested in an ice cream?". After a round of "Hurray", he would drive forty miles to the town where we could get the biggest and best ice cream available. Sound crazy? Yes, but we loved it.

He never forgot fireworks. The week of the fourth of July we would run outside to meet him and look in his lunch box. There were always surprises. Other kids got sparklers but we got genuine San Francisco fireworks – the kind that went 'BOOM'. Sound dangerous? Yes, but we loved it.

Most of the time we had breakfast for dinner on Saturday nights. My dad cooked. My friend thought I had odd parents. I thought breakfast for dinner was a perfectly good idea.

He got up and left for work very early in the morning. He always left silly notes written on paper bags for us. On the day that my Mother was going to do spring cleaning the note said, "Remember, Rome wasn't built in a day. Don't try to clean it in a day either."

My kids are equally blessed because Jim gave them the gift of fun. I think the gift of fun is one of the most important things a dad can do. My kids thank their dad for teaching them to drive, balance their checkbook, make a workable budget, do minor repairs, man the BBQ, and carve the turkey.

However, the most important thing they thank him for is waking them up in the morning with silly songs customized for each child, singing happy birthday off-key at the breakfast table, taking them on off-roads, filling the van with dirt, and making dumb jokes. One other precious memory is that when he sees a new baby born into the family he cries. Silly Ole' Grandpa!

Kids not only say the darnedest things – they remember the darnedest things. Father's day is dedicated to all those silly Ole' Dads and Grandads who gave their children great memories.

CHAPTER 5

THE BLESSING

BECAUSE you might surmise from this piece, I was a starry-eyed young woman who had no idea of life outside the love of my family and their friends. I told this story at our 50th anniversary party to show the true value of marriage and love.

Carla Atkinson

Our wedding was a big deal for a small city. Two newspapers covered it. We had a new sanctuary in our church and ours was the first large gathering since it was built.

Jim and I had known each other since I was seven and he was eight. For many years, his mother worked for my grandmother in the kitchen at Berkeley Baptist Divinity School.

In junior high his family moved to the same area as my family, and they began attending our church. Jim and I were very active leaders of our church group for the next five years. We were also in the same social group – which consisted of Jim, his brother, two friends, and me (the only girl).

Jim had no interest in the planning of a wedding. For a year my mother and I planned the wedding. Because I was raised in the same church most of my life, because I taught the toddler class Sunday school since I was eleven years old, because Jim and I were leaders in the youth activities, and because whenever there was a work day or a cleanup day at church and I was there, the whole church was looking forward to our wedding.

I had many bridal showers, everything from lingerie to kitchen supplies to bedding and fine china. Everything was given to us. Our apartment was completely set up.

My mother designed and made my wedding dress and those of nine brides' maids and hers and my two grandmothers. My parents prepared for and served all 350 guests a full three course dinner after the wedding.

This was my perfect day!

Everything was in place

BECAUSE: A Tale of Two Loves

Everything was perfect

After the beautiful ceremony we formed the traditional reception line. As the guests filed out, we greeted every one. There were many hugs. It was such a happy occasion.

From the corner of my eye I caught them, the only family I knew that didn't have a car. …Uncool. They lived frugally. She was as wide as she was tall. Her hair was greased back into a tiny bun with Crisco cooking oil. She usually carried a parakeet on her shoulder, and always had bird poop on her. "It will dry. You can just flick it off", she said. He was so small that if he stood behind her you couldn't see him - except for his extra-large hook nose, which was visible from the other side of the room. They didn't use deodorant because they didn't want to pay for it – very uncool.

They had a son who wore the same clothes every day – super uncool. The worst thing about him is that he blew his nose in his hand and wiped it on his jacket.

Here they came – to my perfect wedding.

I thought I could just shake their hand and pull them thru the line – as I had seen the pastor do so many times.

BUT NO!

They stopped, took our hands, formed a circle and she said, "As you know we don't spend money on gifts, but I made you a gift". She gave me one of those pot holders you make in kindergarten.

Then she said, "The real gift I want to give you is a blessing". Then she called out to the Lord, "Lord, may you give these two wonderful children the same joy and delight in their marriage as we have had in ours". My first thought was, fat and ugly people have joy and delight in their marriage?

They moved on and our perfect day continued. That day our gifts added to the wonder of the occasion. In all, when we came home from our honeymoon, we came home to a completely furnished apartment – including a stereo and a months' worth of groceries. The only two things we had to buy were a garbage can and a dish rack. Towels, sheets, blankets, pots and pans, dishes, fine china – absolutely everything was there.

By twenty five years of marriage, the dishes were all broken and gone.

The blankets were thread bear.

Same with the towels

The pots and pans existed but had no handles and few lids.

By fifty years of marriage, we realized only one plate survived out of the original gifts.

Now we understood there was really only one gift left.

What do you think that was?...

CHAPTER 6

I LOVED HIM FOR THAT

I also wrote this piece for our 50th anniversary party

BECAUSE I wanted my children, grandchildren,

and family friends to understand the

essence of our love.

People often asked me to share the secret to our longevity.

Actually, it begins with the Lord. It is also about our love and respect for each other, and about our commitment to each other and our relationship. Through the years I have kept a list of the things I love about Jim. I am not poetic. That is what Hallmark is for. These are the things that were on my list, that I thought someday I would share with Jim and the kids. I guess this is the time.

Loved the Lord

When I was twelve years old my dad told me I should be making a list of what I wanted in a boyfriend, a date, and a husband. The first thing on the list was that he would love the Lord.

The thing about loving the Lord is that it puts everything into perspective, and gives purpose to our lives. I recognized Jim's commitment to the Lord when we were just teenagers.

Loving the Lord together has been such a wonderful and rewarding experience, so much so, that we have been able to expand our capabilities for love many times over.

I LOVED HIM FOR THAT.

Loved my parents

My father was a formidable person. He was smart, quick, loud, and funny. However, he scared most people. Jim, in his quiet way, admired my dad and allowed my dad to become his mentor and his second dad. He loved my mom and thrilled her with his manners and thankfulness. We decided early on that our families would be a top priority. So, that meant whenever they wanted us to be there, we would be there.

When we lived by Fresno, and my parents wanted us to come to San Francisco for a birthday party - we went - period.

When we lived in San Jose and my grandparents wanted us to come and bring our six small children to Oregon to see them, we went.

When we lived in Sacramento with twelve kids, and his parents needed help to harvest their almonds, we went.

I LOVED HIM FOR THAT.

Kneeling down when he talked to his sister.

Jim was twelve when his sister was born, so when he became a teenager, she was still quite small. At a time when all the other boys were showing off and when they couldn't be bothered with a younger sister, he always had time for his little sister. When she wanted to talk to him, even if he was with his friends, he got down on one knee and listened and talked with her.

I LOVED HIM FOR THAT.

Not peeling out of the parking lot

Jim has always been sensible – and a little frugal. My dad used to say, "Thank God someone in that family is, and Lord knows it isn't Punk!" (Punk was the Knick name my dad gave me). I never liked a showoff, and Jim was certainly not a showoff. When all the other boys were "peeling out" of the parking lot, Jim carefully drove his car. I am not saying he was an angel, only that he respected the things that he had and took good care of them. He didn't need to show-off to be somebody.

I LOVED HIM FOR THAT.

Laughing at himself

Even though to everyone else he was this extremely good looking, polite, and conservative young man, Jim has always been able to laugh at himself. One time when we were first dating, he bought a milk shake. He was driving a stick shift car at the time, and between shifting, turning, and finding where we wanted to go, he got confused. With the milk shake in his hand, holding onto the steering wheel, he made a left turn. So did the milk shake - right onto his lap. Slightly embarrassed, he threw his head back and let out a great big belly laugh – as only he can do.

I LOVED HIM FOR THAT.

Didn't know he was good looking

Jim has never had a big opinion of himself. In fact, I believe he would be called "humble". When we were seniors in high school he was voted "Best Looking Boy of the Senior Class". I was amused that his only comment was "I think it's only because I am going with you." "Well," I replied, "if that is true then why wasn't I voted best looking girl in the class?". He was taken aback when I brought up my observation!

I LOVED HIM FOR THAT.

Has a new idea every day

He never ceases to amaze me that he has a new idea everyday – at least one, if not more. Sometimes I can sit still listening to the whole idea, and sometimes not, but he never gets tired of telling me his ideas. He is always patient with me if I don't get it right away, and will try anything to explain or help me get it.

I LOVED HIM FOR THAT.

Brings me flowers

I don't remember when he started to bring me flowers. One day, many years ago, he just did. He has been bringing me flowers ever since. Especially when we travel – the first thing he does is buy me flowers. Any special occasion, he brings me flowers. One time my parents took me to Europe for three weeks. He missed me so much he started buying flowers and by the time I got home I thought there had been a funeral. Sometimes Mr. Conservative throws his values right out the window and buys the most expensive thing he can find. He has always kept the romance alive with flowers.

I LOVED HIM FOR THAT.

Always speaks well about his parents and family

Actually, he speaks well about everyone. When we were teenagers and all the other kids were hating on their parents and did nothing but complain about their families, Jim had nothing but good to say about his. Even though his father was sometimes a mean alcoholic, he had no discouraging words. In fact, we were going together for almost a year before I even knew there was a problem. I only knew because my dad told me.

I LOVED HIM FOR THAT.

Aware of his shortcomings

Jim sometimes has a difficult time when expected to speak in front of a group. The thing that has always amazed me is that he will try anyway. When he worked for the Union, and he had to speak as an authority on a subject, or make a presentation before a committee, he would dread the day he had to speak. Never the less, when it came time, he pulled himself together and did his job. He is different from others in that he has no interest in sports, competition, arguing politics, or being "right". He doesn't even care much about being in "style". He likes what he likes and that's that.

I LOVED HIM FOR THAT.

Willing to look within

When we were young Jim had a difficult time with what we call "self Esteem". He was always worried that he wasn't as good as the next person. He was worried that he wouldn't be able to take good care of his family, that he wouldn't be adequate on the job, and on and on. One Sunday the pastor spoke on "In-grown Eyeballs". He spoke on trusting God, getting your eyes off yourself and your shortcomings, because that held you back from all God made you to be. He was very quiet on the way home from church. Actually, he was stunned. He fell to his knees at the foot of the bed and he lifted his head up and spoke out loud, "God could it have been me that pastor was taking about today? If it was me, forgive me Lord and help me keep my eyes on You, not me".

I LOVED HIM FOR THAT.

BECAUSE: A Tale of Two Loves

Built good relationships

When Jim was young, and worked in construction, he was called "Preacher". Not because he ever preached, (he was way too shy), but because he didn't swear, brag, or tell dirty jokes. He never was asked out after work - all the other men went and left him out. Even when he had to work out of town, he was alone. BUT - when anyone had a crisis, who do you think they called on? Jim, of course, because he was a genuine person, someone who wouldn't judge, criticize, or blame. He just built good relationships.

I LOVED HIM FOR THAT.

Peace Maker

Because I am such a strong person it is helpful to have someone who will be honest with me, who will let me know when I am off, or I have gone too far. Jim is great for me because he is not afraid to speak up to me, and because he does it in such a good way, he makes me a more peaceful person. I am usually the "confronter" and he is the peacemaker.

I LOVED HIM FOR THAT.

Loved me for who I am, never said a thing about my weight, and said I am beautiful

Jim gave me a hug one day, and he said I was beautiful. I was having a "fat" day, and I began making negative statements about my weight. Jim held me at arm's length and said, "Don't tell me I don't see what I see", and then he asked "Am I a monogamous man?" "Yes", I replied. "Then", he said "if you are not beautiful, I have no beauty in my life." "That is why I always appreciate that you dress nicely and fix your hair, because I need your beauty in my life."

I REALLY LOVED HIM FOR THAT.

Supported me in anything I wanted to do, and he always encouraged me.

Way back in the days when we only had one child, and the doctor said I would not live through having a second child, my heart was broken. I wanted so badly to have another child, and finally Jim said we would do whatever it took for me to carry another child. I told him I didn't want him to hold it against me some time later when the baby cried all night. He said he never would, and indeed, he never did. It has always amazed me that Jim was so supportive. When I wanted to go to college, he made sure he covered the babysitting. If I wanted to teach a class, he was all for it. When I wanted to babysit, he joined in and played with the kids as much as I did. He made things for and with the kids, and he was a great problem-solver.

When I wanted to go to a meeting to find out about foster care he went with me. When they sent us home with a kid, he was happy about that too. In fact, with each new child that came to us, he embraced the parent roll wholeheartedly. In fact, he used to joke, "I never ask what's new because it usually was another child."

Whenever I made something at the sewing machine, he has always been happy to see what it was and who it was for. He always said, "If we buy me a tool, I use it once or twice and then lose it, but if we buy you a piece of equipment, you fully use it. So don't complain when I want to buy you a better piece of equipment!"

I LOVED HIM FOR THAT.

Pulled the best out of me

Whether it was more education, a better piece of equipment, or a discussion on how we wanted to do something, Jim always pulled the best out in me. When I was mad or complaining, he listened, sometimes sympathized with me, but always looked for an answer, and a way to solve the problem.

I LOVED HIM FOR THAT.

He Sings

Since we were teenagers, Jim has been singing to me. Later he sang to the kids, too. Sometimes he would call me up and sing into the phone. Sometimes he wanted to tell me something and thought of a song that said what he wanted to say, so he sang it. He usually only knows the first line. That's one thing the kids can be assured of. Even the staff in the group home knew they would get their turn to hear a song or two - or at least the first line.

I LOVED HIM FOR THAT.

A tender, romantic, and fun sexual partner

I tend to be a workaholic, as well as hyperactive. But Jim has always insisted that I slow down and let go of my busyness in order to build the loving and physical side of our relationship. One time, many years ago, we took the younger kids and went to our friends' house in Clear Lake for a vacation. We didn't take two of the bigger boys because they had summer jobs. It happened to be our anniversary. Jim had just quit his job with Operating Engineers and we were really feeling down. We had use of the Union car for a month. Then came the call - the boys had stolen our car keys and one of them got drunk and drove our company car between two trees and into the living room of a house. We were devastated! We imagined the worst – people suing us for all we owned, etc. We got all the kids to bed, finally stopped crying, and Jim wanted to cuddle with me. "Not now." I said, "How can you think of romance at a time like this?". Jim answered, "We have lived thru some hard times, but we have never let anything outshine our love for each other. It is our anniversary – time to celebrate!" We did, and that is a good example of how important Jim has led us to make our relationship healthy.

I LOVED HIM FOR THAT.

IS IT ANY WONDER WHY WE HAVE HAD SUCH A LONG AND SUCCESSFUL LOVE AFFAIR?

CHAPTER 7

WHY CARLA

Jim wrote this piece BECAUSE he discovered that

I had written about him. He is adamant that

people should know why and how he chose to

love me and spend his life with

me and over 200 children.

Carla Atkinson

I believe that God chose Carla for me!

HOW IT BEGAN

When I was in the third grade my dad took a leave of absence from the Western Pacific Railroad and accepted a job at the Berkeley Baptist Divinity School as a maintenance custodian. This job included a small home on the campus for us to live in. My mother soon began to work in the school's cafeteria as a helper for Carla's grandmother. I remember many evenings having her grandmother and students from the school come to our house for a visit.

When I was in the fourth grade my family, Carla's grandmother, and some school students were invited to Carla's home for a Sunday BBQ. I don't remember much about Carla on that day except that she and her older brother Jerry and my brother Gary and I were throwing a ball over the house to each other and someone threw it too hard and it landed in the salad bowl on the table in the back yard. Unfortunately, the adults were sitting there visiting and experienced a shower of salad.

I GET TO KNOW CARLA

My family moved to San Lorenzo when I was in the eighth grade. Carla's home was about two miles from there. My mother decided that we would change churches. We had been members of the First Baptist Church of Oakland. So, in 1955 when I started as a freshman at Arroyo High School, I also began to attend San Lorenzo Baptist Church. Carla also attended both. We were both very active in the church. We attended the high school Sunday school class and the Sunday evening youth group. I got to know her very well.

Our youth group had many activities and parties. We went to places like the Santa Cruz Beach and Boardwalk, horseback riding, and roller skating. Many parties were at her house so I got to know her parents.

One time she came to church with a new hair style. It looked really good. This was the first time that I felt an attraction to her. I complimented her on her new hair style.

We had a mutual friend that I had met when I attended the Oakland church. Carla had met her at a Baptist youth conference and became friends. Her name was Ruth and she decided that Carla and I should date. Ruth had lots of parties at her house, which my brother and I attended. I had a girlfriend who lived in Oakland that I would meet at the parties. When Ruth decided that I should date Carla, she started inviting her and tried to separate me from that girlfriend. Eventually it worked but I still didn't date Carla.

I REALIZE SHE IS THE ONE

One Sunday a missionary came to our church. He and his family were supported by our church and he came to tell us about his work in the mission field. He came to the high school group to talk to us. I don't remember most of what he said except that choosing our marriage partner would be one of the most important decisions we would make in our lives. He said that we should pray that the Lord would reveal to us who we should marry.

I began to pray. I don't remember when it became clear to me but without a doubt, I knew he had picked Carla for me. This really scared me because I did not expect to get an answer that quick and I thought I should date more girls before getting married. So, I did not pursue Carla at that time. In fact, I had another girlfriend that attended the same church. Some of my friends in the high school group started telling me that she was telling people that we were getting married, so I broke up with her in a hurry.

In the spring of 1958, our school had a Junior Prom. I was not going with anyone at the time. Since it cost a lot of money, I wanted to take a girl that I felt comfortable with. All the girls that I went with took a while before I felt at ease with them. I had a very strong fear of being rejected by girls. By this time, I knew Carla very well, even though I had not dated her. I knew I would enjoy being with her. She kind of gave me a scare because I called her on the telephone and asked her if she would go with me to Junior Prom. I did not hear an answer. So, I asked again. Still no answer. Finally, I said "Would you or not?" Finally, she said "I guess so!" and hung up.

OUR RELATIONSHIP BEGINS

Our first date was Junior Prom. I never dated another girl after that. God let me know again that she was the one. We started dating regularly and wanted to be together as much as possible. I worked after school but would go see her after dinner. My mother thought we were together too much so I would tell her I needed to go to the public library to study. Carla would meet me there and we would some-what study together.

She told me she wanted to have four children by the time she was 25. She also told me that when she was younger, she planned to got to India and start an orphanage for 100 girls. That should have been a **red flag**, don't you think? I didn't realize what that could mean. If I knew then what I know now, maybe I would have run. However, I would have missed God's blessing.

We both graduated high school in 1959 and by that time we were talking about getting married. Every part of my life from that day on was influenced by my love for Carla. One Saturday in 1960 I made reservations at a restaurant in Palo Alto. I had bought her an engagement ring and planned to ask her to marry me at the restaurant. I was so excited that I could not wait and stopped on the side of the road, just before crossing the Dumbarton Bridge on the way to Palo Alto. I told her to look in the back seat. She did and found the box with the corsage in it. I put it on her and told her to look in the box again. She found the smaller box with the ring in it and opened it. I asked her to marry me. There was no hesitation this time. Carla, being Carla, said "When?"

SO, WHY CARLA?

When I first started being interested in girls my quality picture was someone that looked like Ingrid Bergman and was petite and feminine.

Carla did not match that picture. So, what happened?

- First, out families became friends.
- Second, we went to the same high school and church.
- Third, we got to know each other before we dated.
- And finally, God changed my quality picture to Carla.

We committed to each other before we got married that we would never threaten each other with divorce. We have succeeded in keeping that commitment.

Carla Atkinson

She has a way of making me feel great. The way she looks at me, her cheery voice, and her support of what I think and do. She has given me confidence to do things that I thought I could not do.

Most of the time we have enjoyed working together for Atkinson Youth Services since 1984.

I love her now more than ever and want to be with her all the time.

CHAPTER 8

IN JESUS NAME

BECAUSE I wanted our children to know there was never going to be an end to our love. Because it came from a never-ending source. There wasn't a behavior, no matter how awful, that in the pain they experienced, would cause us to not love them.

In Jesus Name …

We chose to share our lives with you.

In Jesus Name…

We chose to share our family with you.

In Jesus Name…

We chose to accept you knowing there was so much hurt and anger on your part.

In Jesus Name…

We chose to share all our material things with you.

In Jesus Name…

We chose to share all our finances with you. We decided you needed the best clothes, food, and vacations we could give.

In Jesus Name…

We chose to share our time with you. We went to your activities with you, we took you to appointments, and we took you on vacations. We played with you, and we sang and danced with you.

In Jesus Name…

We chose to share our joy with you, and allow you to bring joy to us, even though the trauma you suffered.

In Jesus Name…

We shared our humor with you and still only remember the humorous times and events we had with you.

And finally…

In Jesus Name…

We shared openly our love for each other with you, even though it made us vulnerable to your anger. Because we just couldn't keep such a love quiet.

10620 Treena Street, Suite 230
San Diego, California,
CA 92131 USA
www.readersmagnet.com
1.619.354.2643
Copyright 2024 All Rights Reserved